Business Acumen

90 Minute Guides

Michelle N. Halsey

Contents

Chapter 1 – Business Acumen

Many people believe you are born with business acumen, which is loosely defined as the ability to assess an external market and make effective decisions. Knowing what is necessary to navigate and create a successful business seems innate for certain people. For example, Steve Jobs showed great business acumen. Fortunately, it is possible for the rest of us to improve business acumen. The right training combined with experience will improve your business savvy.

At the end of this tutorial, you should be able to:

- Know how to see the big picture

- Develop a risk management strategy

- Know how to practice financial literacy

- Develop critical thinking

- Practice management acumen

- Find key financial levers

Review the following questions before continuing with the chapter:

1. How would you describe business acumen?

2. Have you ever taken a course to improve your acumen? What was the focus?

3. Where do you feel your business acumen is weak?

4. What do you hope to learn from this course?

Seeing the Big Picture

Business acumen requires an understanding of finance, strategy, and decision making. Most managers and employees, however, are responsible for specific areas, and they have little understanding of the impact their decisions have on other areas. When too much focus is placed on one aspect of the business, it is difficult to make decisions for the good of the company. In order to make effective decisions, it is necessary for you to examine the big picture.

Short and Long Term Interactions

When looking at the big picture, it is necessary to consider long term as well as short term interactions. Short term interactions are immediate, single exchanges, and they are necessary for the company to survive. Without looking at the big picture, however, short term interactions may hinder long term success. For example, you may damage a business relationship by using aggressive sales techniques, costing you sales in the future.

Long term interactions are processes or relationships that are essential to growth. Long term business success requires the long term interactions. The relationships with customers, vendors, and employees need to be carefully cultivated. Failure to cultivate relationships occurs when there is a lack of communication or communication is not respectful. Long term relationships help guide the future of the business.

Improving Long Term Interactions

- **Build relationships:** Relationships must be based on mutual trust, respect, and support.

- **Use feedback:** Request feedback and listen to complaints.

- **Offer value:** Provide value in product, services, and compensation.

Recognize Growth Opportunities

It is essential for every organization to recognize growth opportunities to ensure long term success. An opportunity is any project or investment that will create growth. Opportunities, however, can be overlooked when we do not pay attention to the big picture. Individuals with business acumen are constantly recognizing opportunities for growth. If recognizing opportunities does not come easily for you, there are steps to take that will ensure that you do not overlook growth opportunities.

- **Identify market trends:** Monitor changes in the market such as technological advancements.

- **Actively research customer needs:** Conduct market research and anticipate customer needs, which you will fulfill.

- **Pay attention to competitors:** Take advantage of a competitor's weakness and learn from their strengths.

- **Monitor demographic changes:** Changes in demographics indicate potential shift in customer base or needs.

- **Consult employees:** Do not overlook employee ideas; encourage brainstorming.

- **Monitor abilities of the workforce:** Pay attention to employee skills. Offer training or hire new employees in response to growth opportunities.

Mindfulness of Decisions

Decisions need to be made carefully and mindfully. In stressful situations, it is easy to make decisions based on emotions or external pressure. Recognize these events which increase the risk of making a poor decision that can have long term consequences. Mindful decision making combines reason with intuition to come up with decisions that are based in the present.

Decision making Steps:

Step 1 Be in the moment: Pay attention to how you feel physically and emotionally. This allows you to reach your intuition and understand any feelings of conflict and their source. The source of the conflict may evolve as you become mindful. For example, conflict over the cost of change may shift to conflict that the change goes against company values. Naming the conflict will help you make the decision without fear.

Step 2 Be Clear: Investigate for clarity. Begin by investigating your feelings and identifying the type of decision you are making. A neutral decision, for example, should not create a great deal of stress. Once you identify the decision, make sure you have collected the necessary information to make the decision. Additionally, you should consult the people who will be affected by your decision.

Step 3 Make a choice: Once you have all the information, listen to your intuition, and write down your decision. Take some time to consider this decision. If you are still comfortable with the decision after a few days, act on it.

Everything is Related

In business, it is necessary for each person to perform specific roles and functions. Every business role is related to each other. For example, poor production and poor customer service will affect sales. Too many sales returns cost the company money, damaging the profits. Each aspect of the business relies on the others. Most people only focus on their specific roles, without considering how they affect the other departments. Looking at the big picture allows you to see how everything is related, and it begins with the leadership. The leadership of the company is responsible for the culture and values. These guide the other aspects of business, which are: operations and marketing, finance and governance, and information and people.

How to Relate:

- **Be Comprehensive:** Monitor every area of the business to make sure each one is reaching their goals.

- **Be Balanced:** Make sure that each area of the company is sustainable, and make adjustments as necessary.

- **Be Incorporated:** Integrate every aspect of the business with the others. Show employees how they affect each other and the company as a whole.

Chapter 2 – KPIs (Key Performance Indicators)

Understanding when goals are reached is a necessary aspect of business acumen. Key performance indicators (KPIs) are metrics that show when goals are met. Each company will have a different set of KPIs, depending on individual business needs. Creating and managing KPIs will improve the success of your business as well as your own business acumen.

Decisiveness

KPIs need to be developed decisively. This requires an understanding of which performances need to be measured and how they should be measured. Creating random metrics will not help gauge the effectiveness of your organization.

Decisive KPIs

- **Define areas to monitor:** Determine which areas are successful and which ones need improvement.

- **Identify criteria:** Brainstorm ideas, and use them to create criteria that need to be monitored. For example, criteria would include customer conversion or units per transaction,

- **Define the measurements:** Create specific SMART goals to monitor. An example would be an average of three units per transaction.

Once you have decided the type of KPIs you want, you need the buy in of the stakeholders. Communicate the information decisively and make sure that everyone understands the purpose.

Flexible

While it is necessary to be decisive with KPIs, they must not be static. Flexibility is necessary in every aspect of business, including KPIs. They must change as the goals change. It is important to remember that KPIs can be improved even when they are successful, which means that they need to be reviewed and altered accordingly.

KPIs are often driven from the top down, and they are less effective when the initiative is inflexible. Allow the different departments to adjust KPIs according to their needs, and give them the authority to time implementing the KPIs so that their employees understand and embrace them. Employee buy in is essential to the KPI success. Additionally, coordinating the KPIs on a large scale can cause confusion. It is better to allow different role out times to avoid mistakes.

Strong Initiative

Showing initiative is having the ability take charge over a new or unknown situation. Having initiative is a way for employees to be more automatous in their day to day tasks. It will lead to and produce better problem solving skills. Mistakes will happen, but do not treat them as mistakes or errors, use them as learning events. Taking the responsibility to look after an issue or event by finding the answer, is what having a strong initiative is about.

Developing initiative:

- Recognize spots for improvement.

- Show some confidence, if you have an idea share it.

- Look for solutions, not problems.

- Offer to fill in when gaps occur.

- Don't focus on or get discouraged by mistakes, learn from them.

Being Intuitive

Key Performance indicators can work from the top down or the bottom up. KPIs are created from the top down when they are used in dashboards because dashboards focus on operational goals rather than strategic goals. The dashboard provides intuitive and useful information to users. They require targets to be established for each KPI ahead of time. In order to use a dashboard, all business users need to be involved thus you should interview users to determine the dashboard metrics.

- Which questions need answers?

- Who is affected by the question?

- Why do you believe the question is important?

- Which data do you use to answer the question?

- Will creating KPIs create more questions?

- What action needs to be taken?

- What metrics will you use?

Once you determine metrics, use them to guide and coach employees. Individuals with business acumen understand that metrics should encourage employees to be successful rather than beat them down when the numbers are not met.

Chapter 3 – Risk Management Strategies

Risk management involves different strategies. The purpose is to identify and assess risks and prioritize them in order to monitor and reduce threats to the company. Implementing risk management requires looking at the big picture in the future and taking the proper steps for the good of the organization. Certain risks may be transformed to opportunities, and risk management is essential to business acumen.

Continuous Assessment

A risk assessment will help identify the different dangers and opportunities you may face. There are different types of risks assessments you can implement, depending on the specific objective and the needs of the business such as strategic risk, internal audit, market risk, and customer risk. A risk assessment needs to be a continuous part of the business cycle to be effective.

Risk Assessment Steps:

1. **Recognize objectives:** The scope of the assessment is based on specific objectives, created using SMART goals.

2. **Identify potential events:** Use prior and possible events to determine risks. Identify external factors such as the economy, politics, technology, and the environment as well as internal data. The information identifies risks and opportunities.

3. **Identify risk tolerance:** Determine the variation from the objective that is acceptable with risks.

4. **Determine the probability and impact of risks:** Assign an impact and probability rating to risks based on data.

5. **Outline responses for risks:** Assign a response for each risk. These may be to accept, avoid, reduce, or share the risk.

6. **Determine the impact and possibility:** Evaluate the controls and response.

You should evaluate the assessment to determine what risks are connected between departments and to each other.

Internal and External Factors

Managing risk requires identifying the external and internal factors that affect the company. In certain cases, internal factors and external factors will overlap. In fact, many internal hazards are external hazards. These factors are essential to the risk assessment. The key risks that every business faces are financial, strategic, operational, and hazard. You must determine which factors affect your business and how to address them.

Internal Factor Examples:

- **Financial Risk**: Internal risks include liquidity and cash flow.

- **Strategic Risk**: Intellectual capital and R&D are examples of strategic risks.

- **Operational Risk**: Accounting and the supply chain are examples of internal operational risks.

- **Hazard Risk**: Employees and products are internal hazards.

External Factor Examples:

- **Financial Risk**: External risks include taxes, interest rates, and credit.

- **Strategic Risk**: Competition and customer demand are examples of strategic risks.

- **Operational Risk**: Regulations, culture, and the supply chain are examples of external operational risks.

- **Hazard Risk**: Suppliers, natural risks, and products are external hazards.

Making Adjustments and Corrections

As we established earlier, risk management requires constant monitoring and assessment. As you gather information using KPIs and other tools designated to monitor progress, you will determine which management strategies are successful and which are unsuccessful. Correct and adjust the strategies to improve performance as necessary. Additionally, risks are subject to change. For example, a competitor who suddenly offers a similar product at a cheaper price changes your threat assessment. This will require adjustments and corrections in your objectives, strategies, and actions.

Knowing When to Pull the Trigger or Plug

There are risks in every aspect of business, and not every program will be successful. Risk management strategies help you determine when to go for a win and when it is necessary to cut your losses. Allocating your resources to an ineffective strategy is wasteful. However, pulling resources from potentially successful opportunities may equal a loss. Individuals with business acumen understand how to allocate resources.

Sometimes knowing where to invest is obvious. A program that hemorrhages money year after year, despite adjustments, needs to be cut. Similarly, rolling out a product that has consumer interest is probably a risk worth taking. Other answers are not so clear-cut, even when you have collected extensive data. In these cases, taking advantage of opportunity costs will help determine which risk is worth taking.

Opportunity Cost:

Opportunity Costs are defined as the value of an alternative decision. It is the actual monetary cost as well as the cost of value. In order to determine opportunity cost, however, it is useful to convert everything to dollar amounts. For example, the complete cost of employee training when sales are slipping could be calculated, and the alternative would be the complete cost of not training employees. When calculating opportunity costs, it is important to remember that it is based on projected costs, but it still provides useful information.

Opportunity cost = selected action – the alternative decision

Chapter 4 – Recognizing Learning Events

Every day is an opportunity to learn something new. Individuals with business acumen are able to recognize learning events and take advantage of these opportunities. To be successful, you must always be learning. As you gather knowledge, you will find yourself learning from your mistakes and improving your decision making process. The ability to recognize learning events will benefit you as well as the organization.

Develop a Sense of Always Learning

Every encounter offers a learning experience. The key to recognizing learning events is to develop a sense of always learning. Identifying the eight different ways that we learn, will ensure that you do not overlook learning opportunities.

1. **Imitation:** We learn from observing and imitating others such as instructors or respected mentors.

2. **Reception/Transmission:** Reception is the experience that requires you receive a transmitted message. It may be written or verbal, and it can include values as well as academic understanding.

3. **Exercise:** Actions and practice create learning experiences. These can occur in any action that you practice such as writing, meditation, or computer programs.

4. **Exploration:** Searching for answers or discovering information requires individual initiative. This comes from websites, interviews, books, etc.

5. **Experiment:** Experimenting or assessing the success of a project shows different possible outcomes and influences problem solving.

6. **Creation:** The creative process is also a learning process. These can be individual or group projects. The process ranges from painting to developing a new survey.

7. **Reflection:** Analysis before, during, or after an action is a learning opportunity. This can be done on a personal level or with the help of friends and colleagues.

8. **Debate:** Interactions with others cause us to defend or modify our perspectives. These are potential learning experiences.

Evaluate Past Decisions

Our past decisions often guide our current actions. Both successful and unsuccessful decisions need to be evaluated in order to identify errors in judgment as well as effective thought processes. Ask yourself a few questions after each decision, and learn from your mistakes and achievements.

Questions:

- What was the outcome?

- Did the outcome meet expectations?

- Would you repeat the same decision?

- What information or advice can you take away from this decision?

When you take the time to learn from all of your decisions, even your ineffective choices will bring you success.

Problems Are Learning Opportunities

People prefer to avoid problems or mistakes. However, problems are not always avoidable. When problems arise, you have a chance to learn from them and turn them into opportunities. The first step to learning from problems is to correctly identify the problem. For example, a shortage in cash flow may be caused by loss of sales or unexpected expenses.

Once the problem is identified, consider different solutions or opportunities. For example, a change in the market may provide you with an opportunity to introduce a new product you have been considering. If the problem is familiar, what were your past solutions? For example, did a price reduction help increase sales and improve cash flow? Once you consider the different opportunities associated with your problem, you must make a decision. If you make a mistake, embrace it. If you face the same problem again, you will know what to avoid.

Recognize Your Blind Spots

We all have blind spots in our lives, and they can easily transfer to our business success. Blind spots are parts of our personalities that are hidden to us. They may be deep-seated fears, annoying habits, or judgmental attitudes. Allowing blind spots to persist will cost your company in innovative ideas. Blind spots will also permit ineffective activities to continue. Recognizing your blind spots is not difficult, but it does require the courage to make necessary changes.

- **Request Feedback:** Ask trusted friends and colleagues for honest assessments.

- **Reflect:** Take the time to reflect on your decisions, thought processes, and actions. If you are honest with yourself. You will identify blind spots.

- **Study:** Use books, courses, etc. to help you become more in tune with your views and potential blind spots. Figure out what you don't know and strive to learn.

Chapter 5 – You Need to Know These Answers and More

Running a business is a complex enterprise. In order to look at the big picture in your business, you need to know the answers to some basic financial questions. It is not enough for your accountant to know this information. Business acumen requires you to be aware of these answers so that you will be able to guide your company to success.

What Makes My Company Money?

The purpose of every business is to make a profit. You need to make money in order to survive, but in order to do this; you must identify what makes your company money. You need to examine your products and services to determine which ones are actually making money for the company. For example, a bakery makes croissants, cookies, and cakes. The croissants account for 80% of the sales, and the cakes make up 15% of the sales. Cookies make up 5%, and some days most of them are thrown out. Knowing what makes your company money will provide influence and help steer the future of the company.

What Were Sales Last Year?

Companies need to grow to stay competitive. You are able to identify growth only when you see an increase in sales over time. Knowing last year's sales is essential to understanding the current status of your company. For example, you should use last year's sales to calculate the rate of change.

Rate of change:

Subtract the difference between last year's sales from this year's sales. Last year's sales were $90,000 and this year is $100,000.

$100,000 - $90,000 = $10,000 increase

Divide increase or decrease by the previous year.

10,000/ 90,000 = 0.111

Multiply the rate by 100.

0.111 x 100 = 11% increase

What is Our Profit Margin?

Every business needs to make a profit. The profit margin indicates how well the company is running. A large, successful company typically has a 13% net profit margin. The higher the profit margin, the more efficient the business is run. There are two types of profit margin: gross profit margin and net profit margin. Both are found when the profit is divided by the total revenue. The difference between the two is that the net profit margin is profit after tax and operating costs.

Example:

Revenue = $150,000

Gross profit = $50,000/150,000 = 33% gross profit margin

Net profit = $10,000/150,000 = 10% net profit margin

What Were Our Costs?

A company's costs affect other financial aspects such as profits. This is why it is so important to control costs. Many companies choose to increase profits by cutting costs. However, this can backfire when the costs you cut directly affect the customers' experience.

Basic Costs:

- **COGS:** Cost of goods sold is also called direct cost. This includes costs associated with production, materials, labor, inventory, distribution, and other expenses. The individual COGS must stay below the sale price to make a profit.

- **Operating expenses:** Overhead expenses are included in operating expenses, which is any expense necessary to keep the company running that is not COGS. Examples include support function salaries, rent, marketing, R&D, utilities, equipment, travel, etc.

- **Interest and other expenses:** Interest on loans or investment losses are not part of running the business from day to day, but they affect the bottom line. Other expenses include lawsuits and selling an asset.

- **Taxes:** Federal, state, and local taxes are unavoidable costs of doing business.

Chapter 6 – Financial Literacy

Financial literacy is essential to business acumen. In order to see the big picture, you have to understand every aspect of the company's finances. Fortunately, anyone can improve financial literacy with some basic instruction and practice. This module and the next will provide you with information to improve your understanding of financial literacy.

Assets

Assets are anything of value that the company has that will create a profit or improve revenue. Many assets are listed on a balance sheet such as a building or product. Some assets, however, are not listed on the balance sheet. Assets such as customers and employees are not listed, but they are the most valuable assets that companies have.

A company's strength is determined by its assets, especially its liquidity. A liquid asset is cash or is easily converted to cash, making it more stable in times of emergency. However, businesses are not supposed to hoard cash; they are meant to invest in other assets and utilize them to increase the return in productivity. For example, you may purchase a machine that increases production. The key is balancing liquid assets with the assets you utilize.

Financial Ratios

Financial ratios are formulas that provide information about the company's status. The information used to find financial ratios is typically taken from the financial statement. Ratios are used to find a variety of information, including trends, liquidity, profitability, assets, and financial leverage. We have already examined some ratios in the previous module. The following are some more basic ratios you will need to navigate your financials.

Ratio Formulas:

- ROA (Return on Assets) = Net income/Total assets x 100

- Inventory Turnover = Cost of Goods Sold/ Inventories

- Revenue Sales Growth = This year's revenue/ last year's revenue -1 x 100

- Earnings Per Share Growth = This year's EPAs/Last year's EPAs -1 x 100

Liabilities

Liabilities are money that you owe or a debt. Mortgages or credit balances are liabilities. Liabilities are a measure of financial health. Too many liabilities are an indication that the company is in trouble, particularly if the liabilities exceed the assets. Liabilities may be short term or long term. Short term liabilities are considered mature within a year, and they typically have lower interest rates. Long term liabilities last longer than a year. They are a greater risk, and have higher interest rates.

Equity

Both assets and liabilities are used to determine equity. Your equity, in turn, will determine what type of business risk you are. Lending institutions and investors examine your equity carefully. Good equity is associated with being a low risk investment and it makes you a low risk borrower.

Equity Equation:

- Assets – liabilities = Equity

- Essentially, equity is what you have left after paying off all of the debts that you owe.

- Issuing stocks to shareholders can create equity. For stockholders, equity is what they would have after liquidation. A higher equity ratio indicates that they will earn more money.

- Equity Ratio = Shareholder equity/Assets x 100

- Understanding equity and what it influences is necessary to improve your business acumen.

Financial Statements

Financial literacy requires you to read and understand different reports such as the income statement, balance sheet, and cash flow statement. These internal reports along with external information that you gather, will help you lead a financially stable business. Although it is not glamorous, financial literacy is a necessary part of business acumen.

Income Statement

The income statement allows you to see what money the company made. It is also called a profit and loss statement because it shows the profits or losses for a period, typically a quarter or year. An income statement shows information from the two previous reports, allowing you to determine growth. Each income statement is unique, but there are six measures need to be included.

Parts of an income statement:

- Revenue: Sales or gross revenue

- Cost of goods sold: COGS or the cost of sales

- Gross profit: Revenue – COGS

- Operating expenses and income: Itemize each expense to calculate income

- Net income: Net profit

- EPS: Earnings per share is for public companies

Other expenses and income may also be included if necessary.

Balance Sheet

A balance sheet shows you where your company stands at a given time by showing assets, liability, and equity. Balance sheets are prepared the last day of the month, quarter, or year. The balance sheet allows you to determine the financial health of an organization. While balance sheets are created based on the needs of each company, there are specific topics that need to be addressed.

Items on a balance sheet:

- **Current assets**: specifically liquid assets

- **Total assets:** includes long-term assets such as investments

- **Current liabilities**: liabilities paid within a year

- **Total liabilities**: includes liabilities to be paid past 12 months

- **Stockholders' equity**: Stockholders' equity is used in public trading. If the company is private, equity is the difference between total liabilities and assets.

Cash Flow Statement

A cash flow statement is exactly what it sounds like. It provides information about the cash generated and how it was used. It is also called a sources and uses of cash statement. Cash flow statements are usually generated every quarter or year and contain the three most recent reports. You can use the information in the cash flow statement to define the net increase or decrease in cash equivalents.

Equation:

Cash from operations +/- cash from investments +/- cash from financing = Net increase or decrease

Each cash flow statement is unique, but there are specific items that should be included on the report.

Items on a cash flow statement:

- Net cash (used or provided by) operating activities

- Net cash (used or provided by) investing activities

- Net cash (used or provided by) financing expenses

You begin the cash flow statement with the net income from the income statement, and it ends with the cash equivalent, the beginning of the balance sheet.

Read, Read, and Read

Financial literacy requires continuing education. Do not become complacent in your learning. Read everything that you find concerning financial literacy. You need to read relevant trade publications and periodicals to keep up with the current information. Once you find pertinent information, consider different ways to integrate it into your company's financial strategies.

Source of information:

- Books

- Periodicals

- Trade publications

- Government publications

- Blogs/websites

- Databases

Chapter 7 – Business Acumen in Management

Business acumen requires careful cultivation of resources, specifically one of the most important resources, employees. Managing people is a complex process, but developing your management skills will help you become an effective manager who achieves significant results. Pay careful attention to talent management, change management, asset management, and organizational management.

Talent Management

Talent management differs from employee management in the development process. Rather than abandoning employees to tasks, managers develop employee talent to benefit the organization. Studies have shown that talent management can increase productivity and decrease turnover. There are many different strategies involved in talent management. Below, you will find a few strategies that will improve employee development and increase productivity.

Strategies:

- **Mentor:** Develop mentorship programs, and team up new employees with more experienced ones.

- **Invest:** Invest in effective training programs that develop individuals and make them feel valued.

- **Communicate:** Communicate effectively, which involves active listening and being open and honest.

- **Evaluate:** Choose tools and measures to evaluate the effectiveness of your strategies such as surveys, employee feedback, productivity, etc.

Change Management

Change is inevitable in any organization. Unfortunately, human beings are not wired to accept change easily, so tensions may run high as people resist changes. You can help alleviate the stress associated with change with effective change management. Smoothly implementing change will reduce lost productivity as well as improve workplace culture.

The Process:

Step 1 Prepare:

- **Define the change**: Identify the change, communicate with employees, and assess the needs as well as potential resistance.

- **Choose a team**: Find team members to lead the change.

- **Sponsor**: Determine how leadership will actively sponsor the change.

Step 2 Manage:

- **Develop plans**: Create a change management plan and communicate the details.

- **Act**: Implement the change management plan, and continue to communicate the expectations.

Step 3 Reinforce:

- **Analyze change**: Use surveys and feedback to determine success.

- **Manage resistance**: Understand the causes, look for gaps, and communicate the need for acceptance.

- **Correct or praise**: Praise individuals who implement change effectively, and give corrective actions for resistance.

Asset Management

Asset management is a plan that you implement to define your assets and how they are used. Mismanaged assets will affect your, equity, credit, and reputation. Implementing asset management may be easier with the help of different software programs available.

Steps:

- **Involve the departments:** Determine which departments have assets that need management and coordinate with them. The individual departments are responsible for their assets.

- **Create a list:** Create a list of assets along with the price paid, maintenance, devaluation, and disposal costs. Each department should create its own list.

- **Identify assets to manage:** Choose the different assets that require management. They may be physical, intellectual, etc.

- **Develop a plan:** Use a separate plan for each of the following: facilities management, maintenance plan, capital development.

Organizational Management

Organizational management is unique to each company, depending on structure. It assumes that each singular element is linked to others. The individual unit as a whole must be managed effectively. It requires planning that will lead to company goals.

In organizational management, each employee needs to be part of the plan. You begin with a wide scale plan, and work your way down to the individual employee level. The responsibilities outlined in the plan should fall along the organizational structure of the company. The structure is what links the different positions. For example, there may be regional managers, divisional managers, and departmental managers who oversee different employees. The plan should reflect the distinct divisions. When this is done correctly, all employees will understand the expectations on them and how they contribute to the success of the company.

Chapter 8 – Critical Thinking in Business

In business, you are constantly bombarded with information. You rely on this information to make important decisions. Business acumen requires that you do more than absorb information. You need to think critically to about information and make your decisions accordingly.

Ask the Right Questions

Critical thinking requires you to ask questions continually. You should question people, information, plans, etc. The key to critical thinking is asking the right questions. The questions should:

- Identify assumptions: Is it verified?

- Explore perspectives: What is another point of view?

- Examine evidence: Why did this occur?

- Attempt to understand: What do you mean?

- Consider different implications: Is this important?

For example, a critical thinking question about statistics would be, *"Is this source credible?"* By asking the right questions, you will weed out useless or harmful information and utilize the information that will help you in your endeavors.

Organize Data

Critical thinking and decision making requires you to analyze different data sets. Organizing your data will make it easier for you to analyze. There are programs that will help you get organized. Data may be grouped together for specific reasons, or they may follow certain patterns. For example, you would want to group financial statements together when organizing data. Once you organize your data, you will see trends emerge as you draw conclusions. For example, market trends will become apparent once you organize your research on external business factors. The trends that you see in the data will help guide and shape your business.

Evaluate the Information

You must always evaluate information and conclusions before making any decisions. You should differentiate between a fact and an opinion by using one of the right questions. You also need to identify information and conclusions for any signs of bias. For example, does a conclusion you are reading consider all of the information available? Even when information is factually based, it may not be relevant to the argument, which indicates possible bias. For example, the fact that it was cold one night does not provide information about the lunar cycle. You need to identify facts that are relevant, substantial, and applicable before you draw your own conclusion from the information presented.

Make the Decision

Critical thinking is useful in the decision making process. You already know how to ask questions and evaluate information. Once you have done both, you have a few more considerations before you make the decision. Once you have evaluated everything, make the decision and act on it. You can feel secure knowing that you based your decision on accurate and relevant information.

- **The effects of your decision:** How will the decision affect you, your business, and others? Is the effect long term or short term?

- **Options:** Do you have more than one option?

- **Your feelings:** Are you comfortable with the decision?

Chapter 9 – Key Financial Levers

There are key financial levers that drive any business. These financial levers may be overlooked, but you do so to the detriment of the business. Identifying the levers is the first step to addressing them correctly. Once you understand these key levers, you will increase your business acumen.

Investing in People

People are a key financial lever in any business; people are your greatest asset. The people associated with your business are your customers and your employees. If you do not invest in your people, you are making a disastrous mistake.

Employees: Many companies cut back on expenses related to employees to save money. However, this can backfire and cost you qualified people. Consider investing in employees the following ways:

- Training

- Bonus

- Fair salary

- Relationships

- Opportunity for advancement

Customers: Your job is to anticipate customer needs and wants. You invest in your customers when you offer them what they need. Consider the following customer investments:

- Create new products

- Develop a customer experience

- Improve relationships

Effective Communication

Business knowledge and acumen are not useful if you are incapable of communicating effectively. Communicating is a key to the success of any business, and it begins with listening. You must actively listen to people so that you can answer their questions accurately. Before you begin a conversation, you should also become familiar with the topic.

Communication Techniques:

- **Be honest and concise**: Communicate honestly and quickly with people.

- **Be clear**: Use clear, concise language to avoid confusion.

- **Be polite**: Always answer questions and never interrupt.

- **Be friendly**: Use a conversational tone and avoid confrontation.

Process Improvement

Process improvement is used to analyze business processes. It is also used to introduce a new process or changes to existing ones. Benefiting from process improvement requires you to follow some basic steps:

Steps to Improvement:

- **Identify**: Identify processes to change and prioritize the order of the change process.

- **Establish measures**: Determine objectives and measures used to determine the performance.

- **Determine and validate**: Determine if there are obstacles and the exact path necessary to reach objectives

- **Support**: Get buy in from leadership

- **Data**: Collect and analyze data from surveys, metrics, etc.

- **Options**: Provide different change options.

- **Revise**: Revise the project based on the options chosen.

- **Implement**: Use change management strategies to implement to plan.

- **Approval**: Gain acceptance from stakeholders.

- **Evaluate:** Evaluate the success of the process

Goal Alignment

Part of looking at the big picture of business is goal alignment. Goal alignment is aligning the goals of all managers and employees with the goals of the business. Aligning individual goals is done at the team level. For example, a team goal to increase production 10% over the next month will affect the individual goals.

Team goals are based on the information from cascading goals. These start with goals at the top of the company and change as they cascade down to the different employee levels. Once you have team goals, you can identify your individual goals. Remember, they must be based on company goals. It is also wise to create SMART goals that are specific, measurable, attainable, relevant, and timely.

Additional Titles

The 90 Minute Guide series of books covers a variety of general business skills and are intended to be completed in 90 minutes or less. It is an effective way for building your skill set and can be used to acquire professional development units needed by project managers and other industries to maintain their certification. For the availability of titles please see

https://www.silvercitypublications.com/shop/.

No. 1 - Appreciative Inquiry

No. 2 - Assertiveness and Self Control

No. 3 - Attention Management

No. 4 - Body Language Basics

No. 5 - Business Acumen

No. 6 - Business and Etiquette

No. 7 - Change Management

No. 8 - Coaching and Mentoring

No. 9 - Communications Strategies

No. 10 - Conflict Resolution

No. 11 - Creative Problem Solving

No. 12 - Delivering Constructive Criticism

No. 13 - Developing Creativity

No. 14 - Developing Emotional Intelligence

No. 15 - Developing Interpersonal Skills

No. 16 - Developing Social Intelligence

No. 17 - Employee Motivation

No. 18 - Facilitation Skills

No. 19 - Goal Setting and Getting Things Done

No. 20 - Knowledge Management Fundamentals

No. 21 - Leadership and Influence

No. 22 - Lean Process and Six Sigma Basics

No. 23 - Managing Anger

No. 24 - Meeting Management

No. 25 - Negotiation Skills

No. 26 - Networking Inside a Company

No. 27 - Networking Outside a Company

No. 28 - Office Politics for Managers

No. 29 - Organizational Skills

No. 30 - Performance Management

No. 31 - Presentation Skills

No. 32 - Public Speaking

www.ingramcontent.com/pod-product-compliance
Lightning Source LLC
Chambersburg PA
CBHW071436200326
41520CB00014B/3718